Elegies From the Last Days of the Empire

Elegies From the Last Days of the Empire

Poems by

Jan Worth

Cover design by Shay Culligan
Cover image by Content Pixie on Unsplash

ISBN: 979-8-90146-720-6

Kelsay Books
502 South 1040 East, A-119
American Fork, Utah 84003
Kelsaybooks.com

For my mother, who animated me literally with her body, and with her griefs, longing, and love of the world.

Acknowledgments

Thank you to the following publications where several of these poems first appeared, some in different versions:

Belt Magazine: "Requiem: I Fall While Dancing."
Controlled Burn: "Begonias"
Dives, Diners and Drive-ins, Anthology of Buckham Fine Arts Project: "Cling Peaches"
Driftwood Review: "This World, This World"
Dunes Review: Excerpts from "Lyrics Collected from the Plague" (appeared as "Instead of What Could Have Been")
Exposition Review: "The Hilarious Funeral in LA"
The MacGuffin: "To a Woman in 100 Years, If There's Anyone Left"
The Michigan Poet, Broadside: "Letter to a Childhood Friend"
Qua: "Letter to a Childhood Friend"
Still Life with Conversation: Poems from the Stage Production: "Against Sunlight"

And thanks to Martha Jerrim, editor of my heart, for our hours with the hummingbirds and monarch butterflies.

With deep gratitude to my beloved Ted, for the day we saw each other from that runway in Tonga and our spirits knew.

Amor fati.

Praise for *Elegies*

I've long admired Jan Worth's writing and return often to *That's My Moon over Court Street: Dispatches from a Life in Flint* for witty, compelling essay*s* grounded in the nature, neighbors, and community of her hometown in Michigan.

Worth's newest title, *Elegies from the Last Days of the Empire,* made me think first of Brecht's famous answer that "Yes, there will be singing. / About the dark times." And singing there is in these resilient poems, but an even better touchstone for Worth's clear-eyed meditations and explorations of life under duress would, I believe, be Keats's "vale of Soul-making."

Humble, curious, honest in the face of crumbling empire and "glum outrage" every "frightening day," Jan Worth's deeply felt, closely observed poems (especially the stunning sequence "Lyrics Collected from the Plague") turn quotidian events into guides for survival and self-knowledge. Worth doesn't shrink from asking "Who am I?" It's the reader's reward to find her answer in poem after courageous poem.

—Dr. Terry Bohnhorst Blackhawk, Author,
One Less River and *Maumee, Maumee*

Contents

Against Sunlight 13
This World, This World 14
Sparrows in the Hedges 16
Letter to a Childhood Friend 19
Missiles in Akron, October 1962 20
We Never Thought We Would End Up Like This 22
Black Bathrobe 23
Elegy from a Hard Morning 25
Dinner Party in a Time of Dread 26
Ginger, Garlic, and a Faltering Mind 27
At a Concert When the Music Was Too Beautiful 29
A Storm Was Coming 30
Three Elegies from a Sojourn to the Coast 33
Lyrics Collected from the Plague 38
Begonias 1961 48
To a Woman in 100 Years, If There's Anyone Left 50
Cling Peaches 51
Astonished on the First Day of Pope Leo XIV 52
Requiem: I Fall While Dancing 53

Against Sunlight

Today intermittent light burns
through gloom.
What makes life veer
from its promise, its
brutality of promises?
In this mocking sun,
the world's a blue lover,
bad skin wincing
in the mean great beam.

This World, This World

Sabbath Day after sunspots and angst,
unnatural sun, thermometer a town crier of dread
in this uneasy year. Blooms swell too fast on
lilac and oak, blue scilla up a month too soon
around the backyard Buddha.
A lump in my throat, glum outrage:
how can loveliness like this now make us afraid,
contamination of blessings, and who's to blame?
It may not matter, and how pathetic,
my ludicrous stash of cloth bags
hardly enough to save a single honeybee.
On our walk through early dark,
Vickie points out Venus,
and Jupiter and Mars glint bright,
untouched, a perfect distant comfort
and rebuke: at least our ruin
doesn't reach that far. Vickie says
she doesn't feel safe here
anymore—I know she doesn't mean
our street, green canopy compromised enough.
She means this world, this world, and what,
she says, of the children?
Her husband is also afraid.

Still we stop at Double J's for ice cream.
Familiar drifters part around us,
a dozen Tom Waits at the counter.
Vickie buys me water and
it tastes good all the way home. But even this
is guilt, the plastic bottle
an indictment
warming up in my culpable hand.

Sparrows in the Hedges

I am at an age
when questions fill
every room, cubes ballooned with
heavy air as June gloom breaks up
and my fingers, spiky from
winter's icy strikes
find the keys.
Would they do better
on a Steinway, puzzling out Bach
instead of this box of syntax
and woe? Every day, every hour, every
dangerous blue afternoon?

While the rot of tyrants
spreads over every thing,
daily life still bangs at the door:
city trucks sucking up dust,
slugs in the marigolds,
my body twanging anxiety, needled like
acupuncture gone wrong.
And oh yeah, the meaning of life, my life,
giant bulldozer between me and
tranquility, barging in.

This really isn't like me.

This really is me now.

All winter I considered
going crazy to get it over with,
played crazy and believed it.

Falling so close
to a cold moon breakdown
still stabs me with fear.

And so I murmur

Right, left, recto, verso
What time I am afraid

All the little rhythms altogether

iambic, trochee, anapest
dactyl, spondee
namaste
a mighty fortress
endorphin, cure-alls, tryptophan,

words and words and words
emollients
as the brain calms, as the
spirit sits up, expands.

And so it seems
this isn't the end of things.
While troops assemble
sparrows chatter in the hedges, and
in another room
the dishwasher churns.

Letter to a Childhood Friend

We grew secrets in the sling of a city maple
we knew so well we could climb it in the dark,
and did, arms and legs around the trunk
the truest hug we gave for years,
cheeks against the girth
as if to feel rings form,
our fingers like rock climbers'
poking in for a hold.
At night the bark held heat like asphalt,
the leaves' soft flannel between us and the moon.

Am I a memory you can't live without?
Do you still dream dreams with me in them,
not me exactly but your memory
of being with me on certain summer nights
so shimmering they are like scenes from movies?
Does it sometimes wake you up,
when you feel yourself falling,
the memory of when
you never lost your grip?

What am I to do, my friend,
my heart still in the top
of that big tree?
Did you leave yours there, too,
glowing and stranded
in the highest branches?

Missiles in Akron, October 1962

My parents said
we should get new tires
in case rubber got rationed
again. I caught the scent
of fear. Rubber burned the air,
left dismal grit
on Akron's windowsills.
My mother went to bed,
middle of the day, sleepless,
sweating there for hours.
Rising, she seemed as tired
as before, blanket dents
on a cheek, hair flat on one side.
She left it like that.

I got my period, red splash.
Crawled into my parents' bed,
rare day when my mother didn't
get there first. Nestled
in the pride of new pain,
snuggling it, my own. Got
my first bra, small poking
breasts tender to the touch.

“Little missile girl,” my father
joked. looking at me mournfully
as if I was about to disappear
in some uranium half-life.
“Stop it,” my mother said.

I didn’t believe the world
would end. There was going to be
plenty of time for me, to revel in
my vivid hurts, my lucky changes,
my charmed survival after
my mother and father were history.

We Never Thought We Would End Up Like This

A new friend told me today
over our sweet and savory crepes
in the cozy café that it is Xanax
that is getting her through.
Like me.
She says she cuts it in two,
just like I do. "There is a little line
there right on the pill," she says.
'Right!' I say. We never thought
we would end up like this.
She says her doctor tells her it's okay.
I tell her my therapist
tells me it's okay—in fact, he said,
"It's depressing what you're going through.
Go ahead! That's what they're for."
My friend and I pause over our crepes,
startled that we feel so good,
conspirators adoring each other over the little table.
I take another sip of mocha, which
is delicious. "It's how I get by," she says
and I understand. I take both of her hands
in mine and kiss them.

Black Bathrobe

Is it possible to love
this wakefulness,
cold floor at 3 a.m.,
banister etched in moonlit shadow
black bathrobe pulled from its brass hook,
faint meow of the restless cat
consigned for the night
to the cellar, who quickly gives up?
Is it possible to love
what's stuck in the throat,
what jangles the gut,
what panics the chilly skin,
the need to piss—the body's whole
mystery, paradoxes, double binds,
reversals, ding of the microwave
when the soy milk is done?
Is it possible, fingers arched
over keys trolling for contact,
is it possible here in night's deep cave
to find in it surcease, or peace in
contemplating going
back to bed, where
the worried lover waits?
Is this all about fear, the fear that's
always there, phantom twin
to joy, and loving it as much as
daytime's bright delusions?

A step from the beloved
creaks on old wood floors,
calling an end to the conundrum.
I know which step he’s on—
He’s halfway down.
I meet him there
black bathrobe ready
to wrap around him
before we go back up.

Elegy from a Hard Morning

I took the pill at dawn before I even sat down.
Cupping the hot familiar mug in my hands,
on TV I see three hostages step out of
an SUV, and I am stricken:
how will they keep on living
after all the darkness, the fear, the brutality?
One of them shot in the hand, they say.
What will she be able to hold?
When she looks at her hand or feels its ache, its scar
is there a mother to comfort her?
Is there a child waiting for her embrace?
Will she ever believe there is any goodness left
to answer to cruelty and death?

I couldn't sleep all night
scratching at the pain of existence.
how capriciously comfort slips away.
For now, the warm rooms quiet.

Dinner Party in a Time of Dread

Aspirin and ice water at the kitchen table:
a bath of golden light
in this clean room, the dishes done
and stacked, white rows on creamy shelves.
I lean against the sink to breathe and stare out
at night, the minty air drying my neck and chest.
Fragile sounds—tree frog, cicada, crow—
all tender, everything so apt to disappear.
Somehow my husband sleeps already upstairs, but
I'm wide awake, remembering how, cleaving
to hope, those good people got up
from the long oak table and went home
buoyed for now with blueberries and vodka.

The 1:01 freight out of Chicago
wails over the bumpy Court Street crossing,
and I think this sound we took for yearning
is just neglect—cars rattling with
the cheap stuff we call goods.
Everything is dwindling.

And who am I, sipping water as if
it, I, everything, will just go on?
Night bugs hum. It's time to give up thinking
of eternity. Lieutenants of peace, likely victims,
look at you: bowl, table, platter, window, ladle, mug.

Ginger, Garlic, and a Faltering Mind

I am trying not to notice
what is happening elsewhere,
collapse in the air.
And I am trying not to panic when
he said again and again today, "I am
confused," and there was an edge
in it, his hesitation beneath a shaky blur.

So I rush to cooking,
a recipe with many steps:
smash garlic with the side of a knife
peel ginger, finely chop both,
scent bright in the nose, on the fingers,
peel carrots, dogged scraping,
roll meatballs in the palms,
squeezed tight and round
so the panko thickens.
Chop chop bok choy,
sizzle oil, toss in
meat, carrots, then the roughed up
greens, then the glaze, sweet chili
sauce and OJ and I forget what else
and it all cooks down and boom,
we turn to Jeopardy, his favorite.

But “I am confused,” he says again.
So I sit down close to him and
I ask for his hands and I give him mine
and when I do, the scent of garlic,
the pungence of ginger, is on my hands and I
want him to notice that and I
try to bring him back, bring him back
to this moment in this room and
what we will eat later, what
I made for him on this frightening day.

At a Concert When the Music Was Too Beautiful

When they started to sing
luxurious three-part harmony
in the encircling green room—
womb of hope for a troubled tribe—
when the singers launched measure
after measure, euphony of the spirit,
my own hollow body took it in,
overflow into my ribcage, relief so forceful
it scared me.
I almost lost control, tears
rushing out like music. I wondered
if I was having a breakdown
or a concerto, one or the other.
In the church basement
at the intermission
my mouth was dry and
I took the lemonade in big swallows
and tried to small talk
but I had to get out of there,
up the worn brown steps
into rainy air.
I'd had almost more than I
could handle—finding out
how hungry I am for that
beauty, how desolate I am
for what is lost, how the music
got too close, too close, too much.

A Storm Was Coming

A storm was coming
they said and I felt it
from daybreak on,
something in my forehead,
throbbing my heart.
Times like this, I told myself,
you need a plan.

Start with black Irish tea
made for a friend on
a Sunday afternoon,
and then a platter of
crackers and tangerines
on the coffee table
between us, and then
long gossip while the husbands
did not participate in our
calculations about the
dreadful state of the world.
Just be happy, the one says,
and the other eats another
cracker—all the crackers—
without weighing in.

The little tea didn't work.
In time the friends
left and I walked the
bumpy streets for
the hundredth time
and let benign breezes—

miraculous breezes,
let it be told—gentle
me—the foretold storm
still lobbing chubby
fisticuffs of
clouds to the west.
A woman pushed
a baby carriage.
A woman sweet-nothinged
three tiny dogs
on yellow leashes.
A man with bulldogs
said hello.
Purple crocuses
tucked cheer under picket fences
of Maxine Street.

Back home,
finally the storm did
come through, whipping
the river birch and silver
maple, lashing the lawn
chairs and bird bath.
We sat alert
in our lucky rooms
and counted the
seconds between
thunder claps.

We watched it all,
curious and wary
of the wind. This
time, it wasn't so bad.
The trees stood firm.
We never had to go
to the basement.

Three Elegies from a Sojourn to the Coast

1. The Hilarious Funeral in L.A.

On the way, along Coast Highway
a lone white heron picks at weeds
in the salt marsh, silent apostrophe
in the blunt blocks of condos, new ones every day,
walls of plywood and rebar pushing up
to the edge of the clotted four-lane,
overdone tourists toting boogie boards
and frowns along crowded crosswalks.

I am not at home here.

How can I love where the heron disappears
into a swamp of tee-shirts, street tacos and tattoos?
Jeezus, it's so sad, all the big hard edges, all the
short-lived ripples of the little birds.

In the lush clubhouse courtyard, where people
line up to parse the departed and
nibble catered chimichangas, my throat
constricts again as it has all spring with pollen from
the slutty mulberry, walnut and ash. Or is it the bloom
of mortality in the bleached mid-day light?

I knew him in another life: I was scared of the deceased
until the day he died. When people called him
sonofabitch I thought they meant it fondly, but
I never got it. So I wasn't expecting
so much laughter. My old friend Alan
brings me a cold limonata and, penned into the
crowd of mourning raconteurs, everybody telling stories
about everybody else they could think of—for the fun of it,
for being alive when the dead guy's not,
in the grievously glaring sun—I wrap my hand
around the frosty can and I am glad to have it to hold and
my old friend is saying how he won a prize once for writing a
story about cockfighting and how he just did the whole thing
over the phone. He never set foot in a cockfight and he
says he never would and we are both laughing
like in the old days we shared with the dead guy
who scared me, and my throat is still tight but I
don't care and it feels so good, it's so funny
and I love my old friend and I remember how it used to
feel to laugh all the time when I was afraid and now I'm feeling
great and letting the laughter roll out more, feeling it in
my stomach and my heart at the hilarious funeral,
letting it all go—even the sadness of the fleeting heron.

2. Lost at Angels Gate

—Flyer taped to 20 light poles

Wolfie got lost Sunday at Angels Gate Park.
If you find him, please call me. I am Raven.
Please call this number and ask for me.
No questions asked!
I miss him so much.

The wind from the west
is stiff these days and Raven's flyers flap up from
every pole. She has done her part, but
she comes up every day to look again.
On the cruel deserted hilltop
it is hard to hear when she calls his name:

Wolfie, Woooolfie . . .

The ocean's too big at Angels Gate
the Fifties gun mounts rusted and almost forgotten.
That dog could have run off anywhere.
Three or four of us sit alone on tough unwatered grass,
agape at the sea's metallic glitter.

I put my hoodie up against the gust,
I put my hands in my pockets, ducking
away from the heartless sweep of it, ducking
away from the requiem of Raven's
voice:

Wolfie, Wolfie,
Come back, come back, I am lost.

3. A Reason

Wide open roses tumble over fences
this peaceful morning, wild dill trembling
in the ocean breeze, air so pure
I am breathing in blue.
I feel my blood get redder, my hotspur
skin tip its cells up to the sun. This day
I am shocked by happiness, no matter what,
walking my sprung senses serenely along
the sea, where grasses bend and stand up, where
bougainvillea spills down every wall and eave.

But I am walking with a reason—to see
where a woman jumped or fell, they didn't
know which, on Tuesday. It happened
close to noon, they said—so cruel, full sun.
They found her body at three in the clackety stones
of low tide. I am here to try to know, I think,
how capricious fate collides and cleaves
to what might have been her despair.
The truth in my heart like a sprig of sage:
how those tough cousins, our
hope and hopelessness, can be such
rivals, sometimes depending on
the curve of the rose that morning, the kiss
or the missing kiss of one azure day.

Lyrics Collected from the Plague

Dream #1: I'm yelling Help! Help!
And nobody comes to save me.
My love, my love asleep at my side,
said I mumbled all night—
he couldn't make it out.

TV's nattering heads in this darkened room,
a pestering need to stay "in touch," reverse mantra
agitating the brain, animating me at last to get off
this chair into sunlight, where the only news
is loosestrife invading spikes of yellow grass.

The day is stingy, stingier,
taking back light every dusk.
Sunset tonight, 9:05:
after a hard walk, my body
whines, unsteady,
11 minutes less since solstice.
At the fence,
six careful feet from Ashley, I keep forgetting what
I meant to say. I lean against the
new trellis, a cast-off, cast iron headboard,
curving my hand around the cool metal
of the old curlicues to keep from falling.

Sunrise pounds me breathless,
others' woes not mine, but here they
are inside me: tight forehead
aching. I get up dizzy and scared,
strung out beyond reason.
What to do: open blinds, make the bed,
turn up the heat, boil eggs, tap out
vitamins in case there's a
tomorrow or more: tiny
B and D—hopeful fish oil,
avoid all news.
Daily pleasures don't
stand up to this empty hour.
I hammer the piano like a madwoman,
fumbling what I used to know,
calm myself with Bach,
slow down Prelude #9.
Perched on a kitchen chair
I slip my finger into the little
meter we bought at RiteAid:
pulse rate, oxygen, then
again, pulse rate, oxygen,
pulse rate, oxygen.
They said that might say
if I have it.
So far so good: I am
waiting, waiting
for something to break
I'm not sure what.

Yeah, I'm watching
from my overstuffed chair as
Neil deGrasse Tyson explains
why the sky is blue as
a billionaire takes off.
I don't quite understand the former
and don't care much about
the latter. A bouncy woman declares
it's a religious experience to go into space,
predicts the billionaire might
shed tears. Meanwhile down here on banal earth,
ecstasy a long-gone fantasy,
my gut hurts from eating too much,
and my husband snores in his after-breakfast
nap, and Neil DeGrasse Tyson cushions
a silver and blue globe in both hands and then
from under a desk pulls an apple to explicate
about orbits, and Fareed Zakaria grins and the billionaire falls
from being weightless back to this heavy world. And
Tyson says now can I eat this apple
and Fareed says he can and Neil DeGrasse Tyson
takes the first bite and I suck up last dregs of coffee,
aiming for launch.

3 a.m., the nemesis hour
I lie awake
staring at slats of dark through
casement panes when this barges in:

There is no god
get used to it.
I've never solved
how to replace the soft cushions
of childhood, innocent of that
One who kept us safe. *Put it in God's hands*
my mother's voice—she who
swam herself in seas of despair—
but now this other voice,
At last, *not her:*
You're on your own, take hold.
In the dim bathroom, night light
barely animating my wearied face.
I turn the squeaky mirror
away, pull out the little bottle, squint to see
the expiration date: not here yet.
Shake out one pink pill I break in half,
swallow grateful drafts from the filtered tap
and put at last this godless body to sleep.

September stranded in this life
he's on a walker again.
Tonight, his chair and my chair
pulled close, we talk
about nursing homes, our
eventual end . . . how it would be
the house breathes around us on the

cool night, all the frames of our life
on the walls
like nothing, transient, hardly
ours to keep, hinting at loss.
Helping him get an MRI in the morning
COVID booster in the afternoon.
An old man now, he leans heavily
on me as masked up we stagger in and out of
the discount store.

I walk in foggy, end of daylight drizzle
something calming in it, but I am
bereft. Nobody else out—not
even the five golden retrievers and
their three owners, who love to stop
at the corner of Franklin and Brookside
to chat on the potholed road,
so when I mumble out loud
I wish there was a God . . .
there's nobody
to listen. Nobody to hear.

I reach for jewelry
going out after a year.
I unearth beads, strings of color
from another life, remind myself
how to take the trouble.

Earrings picked for gaiety
the hole has closed on one earlobe
I push the silver hook through:
is it worth the wince?
Then two right hand rings
silver, blue and gold,
(one from my dead sister, one from
a dead friend), then
three beaded bracelets,
for my left wrist, below
my semi-colon tattoo: there
is more to the story.
Going out was scary:
I rush home, exhausted.
I strip the baubles
all off, relieved, and settle down
undecorated, no need to
present. The dead lurking
in these rooms
don't care.

We risk a dinner party:
do I remember how?
Rinse, drain, steam
rice, mix dressing, then
a quick masked run for
strawberries and vodka.

Then to the herbs,
cutting thyme and
rosemary to stuff
inside the chicken's skin
with butter like Sasha used to do.
Sasha who died and broke our hearts.

Then frost a cake, knife smoothing
on butter cream.
Set the table, joyful
flowered tablecloth
napkins to match,
heavy blue plates
rainbow silverware.

Finally I put on turquoise, amethyst
and jasper, and everything done,
I sink into the green chair
with a tiny glass of cabernet
and sip and breathe,
until the long-awaited
chime rings out.
I open the door and
all the much-loved guests
the ones who made it
inoculated against the world
come in.

Stunned by a tough week,
shock of a perfect fall day after all
relief of sleep after all
peace of birds at the feeder after all
(Squawking their flapping little fights)
calm of a perfect omelet after all
reprieve of a good cup of coffee after all
consolation of clean sheets
sailing onto the mattress, flat and smooth,
him on one side, me on the other,
getting it just right, after all.

Here I am again
the same old me, awake,
in cold spring sunlight
through beloved windows:
Say hello, fingers curving
cheerfully over keyboard,
Say hello, matching arms calmly supporting
my hands
Say hello, plush thighs hosting the laptop
Say hello, narrow eager nose remarkably clear
of pollen as the world outside
busts out buds and the lusty doves
lunge at their ducking ladies
who almost always stay one
hopscotch ahead
but not always.

Say hello cranky gut
uncharacteristically
silent this morning before
I torment it with the daily
fare. Say hello, lungs
breathing without me telling
them to. Say hello
oh plucky heart,
lusty beats making music
under my ribs, iamb, iamb,
iamb, sonata with a million
bars, thank you my gorgeous
brain, supplying these words
lining up lining up to make
me smile. I am, I am.

New Year's Eve,
in the "living room," where
we've cowered for hours, days,
weeks this year; once again,
the Great British
Baking Show, marzipan and fondant and
cakes for fun, him in his Lazyboy, me on the
couch where I have feared and
Xanaxed and entertained doom;
outside, guns go off as always
in this troubled town; we watch
as even elsewhere—in Colorado,

fires and fires and fires
the size of Massachusetts they say
and friends in Boulder text
they're okay.
Then it's midnight
and we kiss, his sweet lips still
delicious.
He says I love you.
I say I love you.

We are still here.

Begonias 1961

That year we left behind
a flowering life
(This change was for The Church, I learned,
Or *tried* to learn that sometimes
you must sacrifice)
and in exchange we took possession
of a house of beaten dreams.
A "sunroom" faced the city street with
windows on three sides, rubber dust coating them
gray, and the last preacher's cats had left a permanent
stench. A grand staircase invited beginnings,
but its oak banister's curl was only
a comedown: On those stairs my mother shouted
she belonged in the nuthouse.
My father said she didn't.

In the gravelly back yard by a rundown garage,
my father found porn in a rusted barrel.
Vile and nasty, violent, he said, and he lit a fire
and burned them, bits of women's chainmailed
nipples, obscenely spread legs swirling
just above his head, slick ashes tangled like bees in
his hair, filth stuck in the acrid air. Some thug stuffed
sugar in his engine and stole my brother's bike. Here
he was supposed to find grace, no, not to find it, but
to give it. But he was empty, heretically reading
Rabbit Run and *Henderson the Rain King* at 3 a.m.
instead of his thumbed concordance and the sunny
Gospel of Luke. Finally he settled down with
the Pentateuch, finding comfort in ancient cruelty.

And he bought begonias, the red ones
as red as they come, as red as a battlefield,
as bloody as salvation, and he dug into the
unrepentent dirt, ripped out broken glass
and rusted cans and tore at resistant roots.
He piled in fertilizer and potting soil from
a place in the country, and circled our sad
perimeter with crimson. The begonias' big
dark leaves looked prehistoric,
and the layered blooms like an
upturned skirt, were aggressively
lush. For several weeks begonias flared,
a firewall between us and despair. I wish
I could say they won and my father was
redeemed, but only our misery and the mean dirt
thrived. The begonias shriveled and died.

Today I bought begonias for the first time since,
a heavy pot spilling out the well-remembered
verdant leaves. Superstitious, I picked yellow,
and they sit still in my backyard, a universe
beyond that other hard year.
I see that they are just begonias
they stand for nothing.

To a Woman in 100 Years, If There's Anyone Left

Late spring snow: a clatter
of brittle branches came down. By six
the snow was gone and I went out walking
to see what survived.

Robin in the crown of a locust
riffing into sunset; young pear trees
at the school in bloom, their coifs of white unhurt.
Tulip trees bent and broken, poor lavish divas cracked,
pink petals strewn, final splurge on the sidewalk
at the corner of Beard and Calumet.

Sun a great red ball going down over emerald oaks.
I walked west, then south, then east, then roughly
to the north and back to rosy west, rambling past
neat brick and clapboard, enjoying my geometry.
I like to look at every yard, overgrown yews obscuring
stone porches, new red impatiens in brick corrals,
magnolia splaying last call. I like to look
into the windows of each house, just as the light
reflects off panes, just as soft orange shadows
come up inside. The sky turned pink
as I walked along, the air redolent of lilac
and swampy growth along the creek,
and I savored every breath. The world was still
beautiful tonight. I just thought you should know.

Cling Peaches

Even tonight I am thinking about those peaches, gleaming in their little blue bowl and my mouth is watering at almost midnight and I'm thinking go ahead and want them again, but remember you had them this morning, sitting in a booth at the Olympic Grille with work-weary people shambling around, and when the server sat the blue bowl down, it was so miraculous, like those simple peaches were all that mattered, and I just looked at them first, what a marvel they were shining in their syrup, and then I sliced them into quarter moons and spooned them up slowly, forgetting everything else, and they tasted so good.

So even though I want them again tonight I can't feel too bad, no yearning or regret or muffle of unmet desire rustling at the end of the day, just the memory of those cling peaches, sliding into my mouth and joyfully into my body, how I took in the soft sweet gold, how perfect it was because I had them this morning at the Olympic Grille and how this was a good day all day because of what there is sometimes in the world, how this was a day I got to eat cling peaches from a little blue bowl.

Astonished on the First Day of Pope Leo XIV

Not just all that jubilant pomp,
the white smoke
and Il Papa's kind Midwestern
face, but also, *here:*
a first flicker pecked
into the unmowed spring green
of the back yard,
wild with dandelions
for the bees,
the sun
glinting off his red zucchetto head
and his stately black bib;
and how amazing to be a
human seeing this: how
amazing to be alive to
be astonished by that quiet man
in Rome calling for peace
and the first
flicker in the spring greens
and the bees in the
bursting dandelions.

Requiem: I Fall While Dancing

I'd already had enough
of sorrow, and maybe that's why at the outdoor
show I couldn't sit still on my folding chair
where pandemic style we line up
in a beat-up parking lot, honk for the best riffs and
keep our distance from the trailer stage.
It was old Sam Cooke that got me,
Ramona the blues diva from Toledo stepping over
asphalt chunks to belt from the heart
and also a guy on a three-pronged cane
who staggered out to boogie, grinning and
shuffling to the beat. Who could stay still
for that? Then my friend goes out there,
arthritis be damned, and her man advances, too,
bad knee simply an unwanted comma, and they strip
off masks and ballroom dance
with ponderous charm. An ochre sunset taunts
—cliche of dying light—so finally
I leap out there myself,
circling the others, hooting and laughing and
remembering my hips can shimmy
and I raise my arms overhead and I'm ready to
whoop, and then a woman I don't know grabs me and
we partner dance, backs touching and turning and
we fling each other out and in, breathless duet, but
I know I'm pushing it,
and then, on one heartfelt twirl, I tumble to the potholed ground.

But I don't care and I'm still sort of dancing except lost in the dirt,
and a tangle of arms, white and black, gets me upright and then
I'm embarrassed and I remember I'm old
and somebody hands me my cap and I rear up wobbly but
swinging my hips and wailing into all the grief and
I go on dancing, my body unchastened and
mad and unspent, until the song ends and my thermos of gin is dry
and it's almost dark and I go home bruised to restless sleep,
dreaming lamentations for the millions dead.

About the Author

Jan Worth is a writer, poet, and essayist in Flint, Michigan. She taught writing for two decades at the University of Michigan—Flint and has taught at the Flint Institute of Arts. She was a longtime columnist and for five years, editor of Flint's venerable *East Village Magazine.*

She is the author of the novel *Night Blind* and the essay collection *That's My Moon Over Court Street: Dispatches from a Life in Flint*. Her work has appeared in *Belt Magazine, Dunes Review, Driftwood Review, Exposition Review, Gravel, The MacGuffin, Hypertext Magazine,* and others.

An Ohio native, she is a former newspaper reporter, social worker, and Peace Corps volunteer. She lives with her husband in a big old house on a tree-lined street in Flint.

www.ingramcontent.com/pod-product-compliance
Lightning Source LLC
LaVergne TN
LVHW090537110826
845146LV00003B/1148

* 9 7 9 8 9 0 1 4 6 7 2 0 6 *